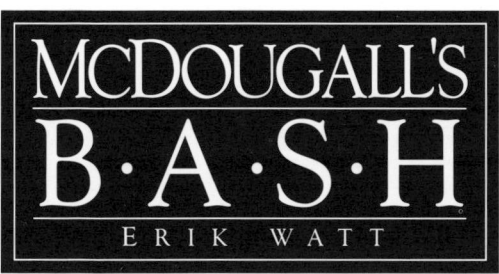

McDOUGALL'S
B·A·S·H
ERIK WATT

Outcrop Ltd.

Yellowknife,
Northwest Territories

Copyright © 1993 Erik Watt

The Joust first appeared in *North/Nord* magazine, published in Ottawa by DIAND; *The Day We Burned the Iglu Down* in *200 % Cracked Wheat* (Coteau Press, Regina); *Nanuq* in an anthology published by World of Poetry, Sacramento, Calif., and *The Prospector* in *yellowknifer*, Yellowknife. They are reprinted with permission.

Cover: Down on Bellot Strait, April, 1957. Temperature, -33° F, Wind 50, gusting to 65 m.p.h.

Canadian Cataloguing in Publication Data

Watt, Erik.
  McDougall's bash

  Poems.
ISBN 0-919315-28-3

  1. Canada, Northern--Poetry. I. Title.
PS8595.A87M3 1993   C811'.54   C93-091437-6
PR9199.3.W37M3 1993

Outcrop Ltd.
The Northern Publishers
Box 1350 Yellowknife, Northwest Territories
Canada X1A 2N9

Printed and bound in Canada

*For Dad, who showed me paths
which careful men should shun.*

To Terry Foster
Best wishes

"Stand to the Door..."

Come in and meet a magnificent, beautiful world with six seasons - spring, summer, fall, freeze-up, winter and break-up - which often seems to be terribly preoccupied with the idea of killing you. And, if you have that touch of insanity those of us who stay here appear to share, fall in love.

You won't meet the whole North here; nor will you learn many of her secrets. What I hope you'll find is some idea of what life in the North has been and is today, in a more or less chronological personal narrative which covers three distinct periods of the Northwest Territories' evolution.

I first saw the N.W.T. in 1943 as a teenage deckhand on the wood-burning sternwheeler Distributor, then queen of the Hudson's Bay Company's long-vanished riverboats (A MEETING ON THE RIVER.) I came back from 1956 to 1959 (ARCTIC SURVEY) as the Edmonton Journal's second designated Northern reporter (my father, author and poet Frederick B. Watt, had been the first, 27 years earlier) and, from 1959 to 1962, as the Winnipeg Free Press' first. And in 1976, accompanied by a wife who dreamed only of escaping (and who'd have to be dragged south kicking and screaming today), I returned again to make the N.W.T. my home (THE SEASONS.)

The events of which I've written happened and the people involved are, or were, real people. Most have only first names, but that's the casual extended family which the thin-populated N.W.T. is. I have friends whose FIRST names I don't know.

One member of this cast - one of our Irish setters - had three interchangable names. He was christened Rowdy Red, and lived up to that, but acquired Horse for his size and Truck for his high-balling approach to life. God is lucky to have him now.

I've written about the sort of incidents most of us have been through up here, not great events... the potential end of the world (DYE MAIN) being one exception. If there seems to be a lot of adventure (defined by a prospector/artist friend, Walt Humphries, as "lack of planning"), there is. You don't often go looking for adventure up here. It finds you soon enough.

And, finally, it took a lot of great people to make this volume a reality. Nick Bakyta and Gail Helfrick gave me the kick-start I needed. My wife, Joy, and family (Dad, at 91, is working on his sixth book), Bob Hornal, Judy Wilson, Brian Lewis, Dave Miller and Dave Lovell wouldn't let me give up. And Dave Lovell, demonstrating the guts of a true Northerner, grubstaked this most perilous adventure of all, with a green poet paddling stern.

E.B.W.
Yellowknife, N.W.T.
January 28, 1993.

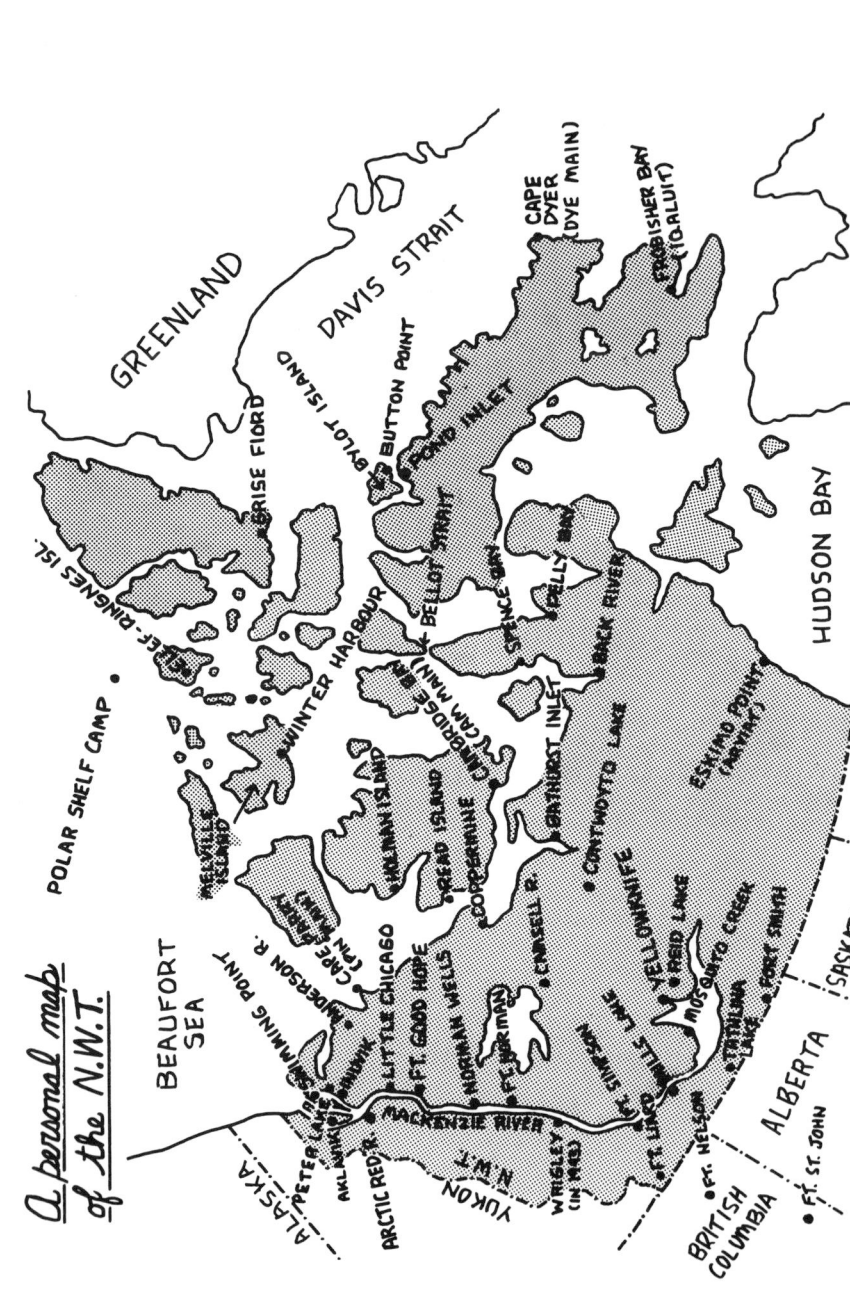

Contents

Northern Spring 1

A Meeting on the River
Milk Run 4
The Seduction 6
Wooding-Up 13
Green Island 15
The Ingrate 17

Arctic Survey
McDougall's Bash 22
Pallak 27
Forcedown 30
The Explorer 32
Trespasser 35
Arctic Justice 38
Dye Main 39

The Seasons
Showdown 44
Lesson 46
The Prospector 49

Antidote 50
Sucker Hole 51
Freeze-Up 52
Crisis 53
The Snowbirds 55
Cabin Fever 56
The Joust 58
The Day We Burned
The Iglu Down 61
Photo Opportunity 63
Winter Carnival 64

Birds, Beasts and Bugs
Skywatcher 72
The Magician 73
Melville Island 75
The Eagle 78
Nanuq 79
The Battle
of Peter Lake 80
Prayer 83

Mr. Holman 85

Northern Spring

We know each other well, this land and I.
She tolerates me and I live her rules
because I love her, not because of fear
(though she is coldly ruthless, faced with fools.)
I know her wrath; I know her awesome beauty;
I know her promise... and I bear her scars.
I know the shrieking fury of her passion
and drowsy peace beneath her firebright stars.

I've trudged her endless Barrens in the springtime
and watched her flowers struggle through the snow
to claim their brief, brave fling of pure enchantment
before the night... and fifty-four below.
I've drifted on her sunlit summer waters
... and fought to stay alive when, swift, she changed
into a howling demon, flailing, clawing,
pounding my reeling boat, enraged, deranged.

She's seared my flesh; she's healed my wounds with
    magic:
a wolf's sad wail; the writhing Northern Lights.
I've loved her and I've hated her and cursed her
... and found in her new strengths, and dreamless
    nights.
I've been alone with her, but rarely lonely,
and she, aloof, and I, in love, have been
companions with a bond of understanding
which nothing mortal ever came between.

And now it's spring again, the time of wonder,
the dark, cold days of winter far behind,
my green-clad mistress calm and soft and waiting
and, youth reborn, pure rapture in my mind.

Yellowknife,
May, 1983.

A Meeting on the River

Milk Run

They'd passed out sandwiches and milk
and oranges before
we hit the foothills' turbulence.
These swirled now, on the floor,
rejected, as the Forty-Six
slammed up and down in frenzy
and skittered sideways 'cross the sky
in search of the Mackenzie.

C-46s were designed
for military duty
and cargo space took precedence
to comfort and to beauty.
Stripped to its metal guts, our plane
reverberated to
each rivet's groan as gusting winds
tried tearing us in two.
Imprisoned in that tortured shell,
we clung in helpless fear
to facing, fold-down bucket seats,
sure that our end was near.

Time often magnifies the facts,
but after years of flying
I can't recall another flight
so grimly horrifying.
We plummeted, were hurled aloft,
were shaken, jarred and battered
five ghastly hours, 'til most had been
so sick that nothing mattered.
Limp bodies sagged in belts cinched tight
while slack limbs flopped and flailed
with ev'ry stomach-churning plunge.
But wild gyrations paled
alongside the miasma of
those half-digested victuals
which filled the reeking cabin as
the Forty-Six played skittles.

Two hours out, our savaged plane
lurched into Fort St. John.

We fueled there and caught our breath,
one-third the journey gone.
Somehow they coaxed us back aboard
and headed north again.

By noon, when Nelson hove in view,
there were no more than ten
whose stomachs still were hanging in.
The winds were growing stronger
and it was doubtful anyone
was going to last much longer.
I'd made it that far.
(God knows how;
I'd never been so scared
so long!)
Now, as we clawed aloft,
we few who had been spared
began succumbing, one by one.
My throat filled up with bile
and in that instant, my eyes met
two eyes across the aisle.
Their owner, a lieutenant in
the Corps of Engineers,
was just as badly off as I,
but somehow grimaced "Cheers!"
I grimaced back.
(You couldn't call
my twisted lips a grin.)
We couldn't hear each other for
the plane's infernal din,
but as we leaped and wallowed in
the mountain downdrafts' grip,
we kept exchanging grimaces
across that reeling ship.
And, somewhere in my sloshing brain,
a stubborn voice insisted
"YOU can't give in 'til HE does!"

And, be damned! My guts resisted!

We cringed amid the retched dead
in nauseated fright
and grimaced at each other for
the rest of that mad flight.

And when... praise God!... we ping-ponged down
on Norman Wells' crude strip,
the Loot and I were two of four
survivors of the trip!

There've been a dozen times since then
when I, bereft of hope,
have felt my churning innards roll
and knew I couldn't cope.
Then, all at once, that pasty face
is grimacing at mine
across that fetid cabin, and
I settle down, just fine!

Norman Wells,
June 10, 1943.

The Seduction

Distributor, they'd called her.
What a name
to give a river queen!
I fell in love
the moment that I saw her, riding white
against the dark green backdrop of the spruce.

Close up, she showed her years.
She bore them well,
and we who crewed her stared in pure contempt
at steel-hulled Diesel tugs which, all too soon,
would force her to retire; to end her days
a lowly hulk, shorn of her upper decks.
But that was in the future.
This was now.

Her foredeck, squared off, snugged against the tow,
a string of barges, often two abreast,
we'd push along The River.
(Only on
Great Slave or in the Beaufort was the tow
a tow in fact, as well as name.)
Downstream,
the tow might be eight barges, loaded deep,

each carrying a hundred tons of freight;
a floating island, forested with pipe
and kegs of nails and trucks and frozen meat
and eggs preserved in paraffin, and flour,
and sugar.
We hauled almost everything
to serve The River's scattered settlements
and help to push the Canol pipeline west.

Right aft, her massive sternwheel, driven by
a walking beam some fifty feet in length,
propelled us at a good five knots upstream
against the strongest currents.
Heading north,
we'd double that speed, or do better still.

The lower deck was ours.
The stokehold, where
Joe Woodsman labored, feeding four-foot logs
into the greedy firebox, and the wood -
stacked deckhead high - took up the forward third.
Midships were galley and the engineroom
(you could have dined on either's well-scrubbed decks)
and, aft of that, our quarters , and some space
for our provisions and essential spares.
My home that summer was the topmost bunk
of three; my music, rattling rudder chains,
two feet above my face, accompanied
by squeaking walking beam and rhythmic thump
of sternwheel paddles, churning up the foam
beyond the bulkhead next to where I lay.

The deck above held cabins and saloon.
There, in a better time, the passengers
had watched The River's wooded banks slide by,
safe from the bugs, and cinders from the stack.
But this was wartime and our guests were few,
mostly Americans, splendid in their pinks,
Sam Brownes and dark brown tunics.
Silver stars
and eagles glittered on their shoulderboards.
Sometimes we'd have a nurse, and, now and then,
an Oblate priest or brother, clergy serge
or brown, rough-woven robe their cross to bear
in the Mackenzie's often-stifling heat.

Our officers lived on the Texas deck,
behind the wheelhouse - captain, pilot, mate
and engineers.
They had the penthouse view.

We never got to know The Wells, although
it was our northern terminus that year.
We'd drop off barges at the Canol dock,
across The River from The Wells itself,
but it was unknown territory, too.
Our home port was in midstream, where we shared
Bear Island with perhaps five hundred blacks
and half as many bears.

We liked the blacks,
if not the U.S. Army's color code.
White troops lived in Camp Canol, with steam heat.
Dirt-floored log cabins, gas drum for a stove,
were adequate for Negro labor troops.

The black troops were a cheerful, friendly bunch.
They came from Cincinnati and Detroit,
but mainly from the Deep South.
Most were men
who'd never seen a snowflake in their lives
and who - at minus sixty - cut the logs
we loaded at the woodpiles on our route.
(Our firebox gobbled sixty cords a day.)
They spent the sunlit summer nights at craps,
where pots were usually a thousand bucks.
(We watched in fascination, as befit
our sixty dollars monthly, and all found.)

Their lonely winter camps, deserted now,
became a summer treasure trove for us.
We'd scavenge tins of butter, juice and fruit,
stacked high and rusting.
U.S. forces might
move on their stomachs, but their stomachs had
no appetite for tinned goods.

Brotherhood
took quite a setback when we green hands hit
the troops' first woodpile; thick, pitch-oozing logs,
greener than we, unsplit and poorly branched

and sixty cords of that to load by hand!
We cursed our erstwhile friends for thirteen hours!
But they, like we, had been beginners then
and after that one pile they had improved,
as we did.
In a month we'd swarm ashore
and stow our sixty cords in four hours flat.

Doc was the eldest deckhand, seventeen
and waiting for the fall, when he'd enlist.
Twit was a farm boy, and he was in shape
for heavy work.
We other six had thought
that we were pretty tough sixteen-year-olds...
until that first day when we wooded-up.
We were to sail that night.
We slept, instead,
exhausted, bleeding, full-clad, where we dropped,
in my case, half-across my upper bunk,
my booted feet suspended in mid-air.

We never spent much time ashore that year.
There was a war, and Canol needed pipe,
and we were there to barge it from Mills Lake,
a fly-infested U.S. Army camp,
carved from the bush five hundred miles upstream.
There, tons of pipe and other stores, hauled north
by tractor train along a winter road,
made clear why we ate four full meals per day.
A four-month navigation season meant
we worked until the cargo was aboard,
an hour for meals, ten minutes every hour,
the only breaks we'd get.

Once under way
we'd catch up on the sleep which we had missed.

❖   ❖   ❖

The settlements were different.
They dozed
beneath a Midnight Sun which never set
and spread thin arms along the riverbank
to catch its warmth.
At first, we wondered why

the Hudson's Bay, the missions and police
and Army Signals Corps compounds should sit
so far apart.
The answer, as we learned,
was that the whites who lived here had come north
to get away from crowded city life
... and elbow room, the Territories had.
Yet, rugged individuals or not,
whites matched the natives' hospitality.
The coffee pot was always on the stove,
and no one ever knocked.
You just walked in
and poured yourself a cup before you joined
whoever else might happen to be there.

(In later years, I learned to pour a shot
which, liquor being scarce, was quite an art.
No host would measure out your drink himself;
the bottle sat there, and you poured your own.
Too little, and your host would be upset
to think you thought him miserly.
Too much,
and you were branded as a greedy sod.)

There were divisions.
Few whites went to church
(too regimented for their freemen's souls)
and there was little ecumenical
about the priests and ministers.
They vied
for converts, and they did their level best
to keep their flocks apart, lest some should stray
into the other camp.
And yet it was
the churches which provided both the schools
and hospitals for those of every creed.

The trappers, mostly Slaveys, quite enjoyed
the whites' odd feuds, and subtly egged them on,
though baffled by that love of privacy.
Their cabins snuggled close.
Out in the bush
in winter, they had solitude to spare.

They might not see another face, except
at Christmastime and Easter, for eight months.
When summer and its ruthless flies arrived,
they congregated happily "in town,"
to catch up on the gossip they had missed
or do a bit of fishing, or just sit
atop the riverbank, and let the sun
work healing wonders on their winter aches.

"Flies" covered everything which flew and bit;
mosquitoes, no-see-ums, blackflies; the lot.
Their humming millions made the summer bush
a horror for the hapless traveler.
Our nemesis was bulldogs.
Our first trip
we pushed a barge of furs from Fort Good Hope
and never lost its host of carnivores,
huge super-horseflies which removed a chunk
of flesh each time they hit you.
Weeping sores
which itched for days were worse than blackfly bites.
(I well recall one woodpile by a swamp
which shimmered with mosquitoes, wing-to-wing,
and thinking, as they settled in to feed,
how nice it was to be so gently bled!)

Most claim the aircraft opened up the North.
Muskol, the fly repellent, gets MY vote!

Fort Simpson, Wrigley and Fort Norman were
the only settlements along our track
and brief forays ashore, unloading freight,
left little time for gawking.
Yet we all
soon felt the closeness Northern people shared,
despite their superficial bickering.
Four Slavey deckhands joined us later on,
lithe, strong young men who didn't talk a lot
but taught us how to learn by listening.

And so that summer on The River passed.
Flab became sinew; carefree schoolboys, men,
and an adventure, something more than fun.
Much of our wisdom came the hard way.

We
learned soon enough that beauty was skin-deep;
that on this frontier, wise men stayed alert;
that men must trust each other... and themselves.
The work was hard; the money, poor.
The pay
which counted was the bond of comradeship
to which, once we had paid our dues, we were
admitted...
and, beneath it all, there pulsed
the constant challenge of the North herself.

To some she was a feeling, nothing more;
a sense of awful menace; waiting, set
to strike the instant that your guard was down;
something to get away from while you could.

But not to me.

To me she was a siren, beautiful
beyond belief... or any mortal's grasp...
taunting and teasing, playing deadly games
and daring you to meet her, face-to-face.

We met the first time in a swirling fog
out on The River; just the two of us.
I didn't even know that she was there.
But later, quaking in my bunk, I knew,
and suddenly my draining fear was gone,
lost in a flood of foolish, surging pride
which made me voice my feeble boast aloud:

"I beat you this time!"

And I knew I had.

And, heading Out that fall across Great Slave,
I somehow knew that one day I'd be back.

Great Slave Lake,
September, 1943.

Wooding-Up

Raw new clearing
up ahead,
boiler panting
to be fed.
Twenty hours
under way;
time for wooding-
up today.

Lead barge grounded
'neath the bank,
dance ashore
on wobbly plank
with the bow line.
Paddles churn
'til you get
a double turn
'round a treetrunk,
make it fast.
Engines can
relax at last.

Swing in snugly
to the beach.
Gangplank out
when it will reach.
Stern secure
and crew ashore,
up the bank
to load once more.
Jolly priest
has joined the crew
(Passengers
quite often do.)

Four feet long, piled
four feet high,
watch the heavy
spruce logs fly
fifty feet to
beach below

'til there's sixty
cords to stow.

Form a line from
pile to ship.
Start the logs up.
Gloved hands flip
flying cordwood
on its way
'til one cocks...
then, hell to pay!

Four-foot missile,
tumbling wild,
knocks priest over!
Air defiled
as the cassocked
victim lands
in The River!
Grinning hands
drag the cursing
priest ashore.
(He will volunteer
no more!)

Flip! - flip! - flip!
The hurtling wood,
barely touched,
flows, as it should
up the gangplank,
past the pit,
to be stacked.
Then, pause a bit.

Line moves up.
Two others take
woodpile end
to give a break
to the pair
who start the chain.

Back to passing
logs again.

Four hours later,
task complete,
paddlewheel
resumes its beat.
Joe the fireman
stokes his blaze
with the logs
I feed him.

Haze
blurs the steep banks
gliding past.
Two more hours and
bunk, at last!

*On The River
near Wrigley,
July, 1943.*

Green Island

I took off unobserved, in fog so thick
you couldn't see ten feet.
I can recall,
quite vividly, the thought which came to mind:
that one should never take a turn of line
about one's hand, when dipping overside
to get a pail of water.

Of the flight
itself, I have no memory at all;
nor of the landing, though it must have jarred.

Now, here I was; my left boot tightly wedged
into a deck cleat, body twisted back
towards the stern, at forty-five degrees,
held rigid by the rope wrapped 'round my palm
and fastened to the bucket, dragging hard
against the rapids' current.

Boy, I thought,
That REALLY was a stupid thing to do!

There was no sound at all, except the hiss
of seething water slipping past the hull
and, from the fog astern, the THUMP!-THUMP!-THUMP!
of sternwheel paddles, digging in to fight
the six-knot current.

I was quite alone.

Somewhere above me, in the pilothouse,
our pilot, Johnny Berens, sniffed the course
as he had done for forty years or so.
The River was HIS country.
Fog or shine,
he'd con us through without a single scrape,
although Green Island channel's snaking track
meant barges must be relayed, one by one.
Beside him, Captain Naylor, cool, alert,
and Johnny's grandson, learning Grandpa's craft.
Ten paces inboard, in the fireman's pit,
Joe Woodsman, naked torso slick with sweat,
would be relaxing by the firebox now
and waiting for the drink I'd gone to fetch.

Joe wouldn't hear me, though they would above,
but yelling "Help!" had never crossed my mind.
It was, at this point, calmly calling up
the stories I had heard of people who
had made the passage through the sternwheel's blades.

I was deciding I would rather not,
and that I'd better think of getting free.

It wasn't easy.

All I had to do
was twist my hand palm-upward, so the coil
of line could loosen, and the turn yank free.
The problem came in making that small move
against The River's pull.
It didn't want
to let me go, now that it had me hooked.

That made me mad.
Somehow I grabbed some slack
and flipped my wrist, and felt the snaking line
burn hot across my palm, and disappear

into the swirling fog as I, released,
fell overside.
I think my fingers brushed
the water then, although I'm not quite sure.
Nor have I any recollection how
I grabbed the cleat which held my foot, and then
managed to haul my body back aboard.

I do remember standing on the deck
and thinking I'd catch hell because I'd let
the bucket go; then wandering inside
to pass more logs to Joe.

Some minutes passed
before Joe asked me "Where the hell's my drink?"
and I sat down upon the deck, and shook,
and Joe found someone else to work my watch.

Near Fort Simpson,
July, 1943.

The Ingrate

"Man overboard!"

Only the Captain saw
the accident.
His eyes were everywhere.
We, sailing soon, were busy checking lines
when the departing boat cut sharp, broached to
and flipped them in The River, swift and cold.
I caught a glimpse - a head, some bobbing tins,
the boat, still running - racing up towards
the Texas deck, where all our boats were slung.

We'd never had a boat drill, but the Mate
was there.
The boat swung out with lightning speed
while some of us ran down to man it.

Then,
as it came creaking down the falls, we found
the whaler only held one set of oars.
Mel and I leaped aboard, just as the Mate

came whistling down the falls, hands scorching raw,
and we were in the water, rowing hard,
before we'd even had a chance to think
of how the davit lines should be released.
(Adrenalin takes care of small details.)

The current's really swift at Norman Wells.
We saw a floating box and other junk,
but of the two men, nothing.
Then the Mate,
who'd shipped the rudder, and was steering, yelled
"Pull port!" and headed us towards one man
who floundered in The River's icy clutch.

He neither saw nor heard us as we neared,
though we were shouting to him as we pulled,
afraid he'd vanish just as help arrived.
His voice was nearly gone.
His bulging eyes
stared through as us he turned towards the boat,
arms weakly flailing, hollering for help.
I dropped my oar as we drew near, stood up
and started peeling off my shirt.

"Stay put!
"Just grab him!" roared the Mate.
And so I did...
and nearly finished him, right there and then!
I vaguely knew you seized a drowning man
securely by the hair... but he was bald!
And so I grabbed his parka, which had trapped
sufficient air to help him keep afloat
and, as our boat slid past, near strangled him,
pulling the parka tight across his neck!

We couldn't haul him inboard.
He was fat
and waterlogged, and couldn't help himself.
We hooked him on the gunwale by his arms
and held him as we searched The River for
a sign of his companion.

There was none.

"We'd better get this guy to shore, and fast,"
the Mate said, finally.
His voice was flat,
and all at once we three became aware
of just how tired we were.
My body ached.
The oar I pulled on seemed to weigh a ton,
and I was quite surprised to hear the keel
grate on the gravel beach.
We had despaired
of ever reaching shore.
What strength we had
was finished by the time the three of us
had dragged the lone survivor to the beach
and Captain Naylor, casting off the tow,
had drifted down a mile to pick us up.

Our prize was a civilian Canol boss.
The chap who drowned, an Indian named Boots,
would have found time to thank us afterwards.

Bear Island,
August, 1943.

Arctic Survey

McDougall's Bash

McDougall is retired by now
and Bill is long since dead
and Sid no longer flies, and so
it's safe to go ahead
and tell about Sid's epic flight
through ice and snow and fog
from Coppermine to Yellowknife...
and what's NOT in the log.

In 'Fifty-seven, no one knew
of oil beneath the ice
and health care for the Eskimo
was governed by its price.
So, once a year, in Ottawa
the government would spring
for one Health charter, out of Cam.
It handled everything
from medicals to dental work
and X-rays, tests and shots
on DEW Line sites, in settlements
and Godforsaken spots
along the Central Arctic coast
from Pin to Pelly Bay.
And where the Arctic Survey flew,
Bill Davies led the way.

Doc Davies hated aeroplanes
...and flew that route each year
for Health and Welfare.
Dr. D.'s
compassion conquered fear.
A dentist, three MDs, three techs;
up front, a guide and Sid;
six hundred pounds of gear, full tanks...
My God! The things we did
before the days of strips and fuel
and beacons everywhere,
when Single Otter pilots flew
on skill and guts and prayer!

We flew from Cam to Pelly Bay,
to Bellot Strait, and then

to Bathurst Inlet, Holman, Read,
Pin Main and back again.
For thirty days, we rarely saw
the ground, once in the air,
(and cabin heat or radio
seemed our two choices there.)
We'd fly at daybreak - half-past six -
and stagger in at night
so wiped we'd often fall asleep
before we'd had a bite.

We held our clinics where we could,
in schools and trading posts,
an iglu, churches, storage sheds -
and bunked in with our hosts.
On DEW Line sites, we slept in beds.
Most times, we used the floor.
We might set up three times a day;
check people by the score.
(Our record was 250 in
a single day at Cam.
It took us 'til 11 p.m.
to clear THAT traffic jam!)

Our overload was bad enough
if April had been fine.
It wasn't.
White-outs, blizzards, fog
were ours, all down the line,
and knifing winds, and temps. which hit
a low of forty-four,
rough sea ice strips - where there WERE strips -
and, every day, some more.
Frost-bitten, gaunt from lack of sleep
(the legacy of fear),
at last we were in Coppermine
and almost in the clear.

We had just one more camp to see,
down at Contwoyto Lake,
and Mac, the Mountie corporal,
urged Bill to take a break.
"I've got a case of rum," he said,
"and your gang's earned a bash.

"Why don't you all drop in tonight
"and join me for a smash?"
Bill was as beat as anyone
and saw no reason why
we shouldn't.
Thirty nightmare days
leaves anybody dry.

❖ ❖ ❖

I don't recall McDougall's bash
in any great detail,
except that I awoke next day
feeling exceeding frail.
I know we were a quiet crew
at breakfast, which some ate,
Bill'd turfed us out of bed at five;
HIS flights did not leave late.
and while McDougall's bash had purged
our systems of their strain,
the cure had nearly done us in,
as bleary eyes made plain.

Sid had already left, to thaw
the frozen aircraft out
and check the weather, long before
we laggards were about.
We tottered out into the dawn
like Bonaparte's Retreat
and winced at Sid's cheer greeting:
"Well!
"Radio or heat?"
We'd rarely had the luxury
of having both, and so
we told him we'd take cabin heat
as we prepared to go.

❖ ❖ ❖

Contwoyto was a nasty place
to find when things were good;
its beacon functioned now and then,
but rarely when it should,
and we were flying into Spring.
The temp'rature was nice,

but one above is also where
clouds tend to fill with ice.
Still, we were heading home, and though
the weather swift declined,
the thought of turning back did not
cross anybody's mind.

Below were the Septembers,
the rugged mountains which
lie waiting on a pilot's path
to Yellowknife.
You twitch
to see them eye you hungrily
(no place down there to land)
and if Contwoyto's out, you can
have trouble close at hand.
And that we had, this April day,
the ceiling coming down,
the mountains coming up, and Sid
wearing a troubled frown.
"I doubt we can get back," he yelled
above the engine's roar.
"Contwoyto's out.
"We can't sit down.
"I guess you know the score."

Indeed we did.
Below, the rock.
Above, the ice.
We knew
the Otter lacked de-icing gear.
Could we just luck it through?
The mountains helped us to decide;
our chances there were nil.
"Okay, then.
"Take her up.
"We'll have
"to chance the ice," said Bill.
Sid hauled back on the wheel, and we
climbed up into the klag.

We started icing instantly
and felt the Otter flag.

Up... up... we fought and, knot by knot,
our airspeed dropped until
our wings, our tail, our fuselage,
our prop were glazed!
And still
Sid struggled to maintain our climb,
sweat running down his face,
coaxing the lurching Otter through
that hellish piece of space.

Four thousand feet we staggered up,
our aeroplane a brick
encased in ice, which Sid could see
had built a half-inch thick
upon the straining, tortured prop
and then...
Thank God!
The sky!
Bright sunlight sparkled on our wings.
Lord, how that man could fly!
Great chunks of ice went whipping past
the windows as we fled
toward the south, the stormclouds' edge
just visible ahead.

The rest was anticlimax as
Sid set the Otter down
on Back Bay's ice, and taxiied to
the dock in Lower Town.
"I think I need a drink," I said
as I released my belt,
and Sid admitted that he knew
exactly how I felt.
We drove up to the New Town, where
we fell into the bar
and summonsed Ruby, and a round
to toast our lucky star.
The rum cascaded down my throat
in one convulsive GLUMP!
and, slowly, I could feel my heart
resume a normal thump.
"I need another, Sid," I said.
"It's been a trying trip!
"One more for you?"

Sid leaped erect.
I swore that he would flip!

"Shucks, no!" he said.
"I gotta quit!
"I'd really like to stay,
"but my alarm is set for four.
"We're flying home today!"

❖   ❖   ❖

We fly from strip to strip, these days,
on wheels, not floats or skis,
though flying still has moments when
your heart's inclined to freeze.
But no cold panic's ever matched
the terror which was mine
when I discovered Sid still thought
he was in Coppermine!

Yellowknife,
April, 1957.

Pallak

He crawled into the iglu, grinning through
the ice which caked his moustache.
Twinkling eyes
lit up his dark-skinned, lined and weathered face
and, as he straightened up, we saw we'd found
the man we all had hoped to meet - Pallak.

He was a legend on the Queen Maud coast.
Five years before, out hunting on the ice,
he'd blown his leg half-off below the knee.
Back River camp was fifty miles away,
two days by dogteam over jumbled floes,
and Pallak knew his mangled leg would sap
his strength on that grim journey.
So he took
his skinning knife and, concentrating hard,
removed the mess his rifle slug had left,
bound up the stump and drove his huskies home.

When summer came he found a piece of wood,
washed down the river to the treeless coast,
and carved himself a leg.
Two willow sticks
formed braces up the sides, and thongs secured
his pegleg to his stump.
The final touch,
a pad of muskox horn, pegged to the base,
preserved the precious wood from rocky ground.

The doctors in our party knew of him,
but none had ever met this man, or seen
the leg which made him famous.
Now they stared
in admiration at his neat-sewn stump
(he'd left a flap of skin to shield the bone)
and at his artificial leg, on which
no fancy metal limb could much improve.
And Pallak, though he spoke no English, beamed
to see approval in the experts' eyes.

I thought of Pallak often in the year
which passed before I heard of him again,
and what a tough old bird he was, and how,
on one leg and a peg, he dared a land
which killed whole men with bland indifference.

And then I met the priest from Pelly Bay
and learned just what a man he really was.

That winter had been hard.
The caribou
came nowhere near Back River.
Food was scarce,
so Pallak and his family - his son,
his son's wife and their twins, just five years old,
had ventured far out on the ice for seal.
Bad weather caught them there, their food all gone.
They'd found no seals; the ice was far too thick.
That meant no fuel for their soapstone lamp,
the *kudlik*, used for cooking, light and heat.
Inside their iglu they were safe, if cold,
but hunger shared the fur-spread sleeping bench
on which they huddled close, conserving warmth,
while, outside, certain death crouched in the gale.

The first storm lasted five days, then the next
swept in before they'd made a dozen miles.
They killed their starving huskies, one by one,
and lived on them until the raging wind
blew itself out.
By then, all five were weak
from hunger and the unrelenting cold...
and facing sixty miles of dragon's teeth
formed by the pressure ridges on the ice.

They pushed themselves towards the distant camp,
their hunger secondary now to thirst.
They had no fuel left with which to melt
the hard-packed snow whose endless miles they trudged
and snow, scooped up and eaten, merely feeds
your agony... or freezes lungs and guts
in bitter cold like that.
Each day, they made
a few more miles, the best that they could do,
parched, hungry, half-delerious and chilled.

The morning of their last day, Pallak woke
to hear the children crying for a drink.
He couldn't stand their tears.
He took his leg
and chopped it into kindling for a fire
to melt some snow and ease their suffering.
He knew they'd little chance of reaching camp
and he, on one leg, stood no chance at all -
but what grandfather lets a grandchild cry
when there is something he can do to help?

Two hours later, Father Van de Velde,
making his yearly journey to the Back
from Pelly Bay by dogteam, came upon
five starving Inuit and took them home.

❖   ❖   ❖

God keeps an eye on sparrows, we are told,
and watches little children as they sleep.

He obviously loves grandfathers, too.

Back River,
April, 1958.

Forcedown

"Mayday... Mayday..."

Sid's calm voice
gives no hint of fearful choice:
find the ice, or turn and run
... and hope it's clear when fuel's done.

"J-A-O to Spence or Cam..."

Weather's put us in this jam,
weather, plus a radio
dead at least an hour ago.
We're transmitting, we believe,
but there's nothing to receive.

Not a cloud in sight at dawn,
then - our flying range half-gone -
blizzard over Bellot Strait
and receiver out!
Too late,
now, to try Spence Bay and find
weather's just as bad behind
when we get there.
Empty tanks
make for poor blind landings, thanks!

Boothia's crags, like islands, float
above the klag.
Sid's quiet rote
continues:

"We're descending now..."

If his call gets through somehow,
searchers will know where to look,
should our Pilot close the book.

Bellot is a mile-wide gap
amid the rock; we need no map.

Down...
    down...
        down...

Four thousand...

Three...

Turbulence...

At first, we see
our shadow on the swirling cloud,
but then the snow becomes a shroud,
impenetrable by the sun...

Two thousand...

Fifteen hundred...

One...

And down we sink, in growing dread,
opaque nothingness ahead.
Are they reading Sid down there
as, swiftly, we run out of air?
Somewhere in this seething murk
rock... and open water... lurk...

Seven hundred...

Six...

Now, four...
Can our nerves take any more?

Three...

Two-fifty...

Two...

Eyes lock
on the fast-unwinding clock.

Nothing!
Does the klag extend
clear down to the ice?

The end?

Seventy...

Sixty...

Sudden cheer!
Ice below!
We've broken clear!

"... Touching down..."

"We're down, all right.
"Looks as if we'll spend the night..."

One more entry for the log:
"Forced to land in snow and fog."

*On the Boothia Peninsula,
April, 1957.*

The Explorer

"JUDITH!"

The River, muttering as it swirls
toward the distant Beaufort, pays no heed.

"JU-DITH!"

The black spruce forest, marching down
to meet the narrow beach, ignores me, too.

"JUUU-DITH!"

Not even echoes, where a moose
could crash in silence through the undergrowth

which swallows every sound, except the thump
of one despairing father's pounding heart.

One moment she was scratching at her bites,
a band of scars about her chunky waist
where jeans and tank top never did quite meet.
Next instant, she was gone - I thought - to join
her sister and her mother on the beach.
There, we had set our tent up for the "night,"
those magic hours in which the Midnight Sun
splashes its golden warmth on tree and rock
and burnishes the mile-wide River's face.

And now...
Oh, God!
She's lost!
A hundred miles
from Good Hope; farther yet from Arctic Red!
And I... .I brought her here, despite the pleas
of friends and relatives who paled to think
we'd take kids, five and six, a thousand miles
down the Mackenzie for a holiday.

"JUDITH!"

The River holds no fear for her.
She's taken storms and crises in her stride,
often asleep beneath the flailing tarp
when things were rough.
In every settlement
our five-year-old has easily acquired
a retinue of friends, who show her how
to clean a fish, or how the furs are stretched,
or take her home for bannock and some tea.

"JUDITH!"

How real delight lit up her face
amid the tossing whitecaps of Sans Sault,
the only rapids worthy of the name
along The River's length!
Our spinning boat,
its kicker swamped, was my concern, not hers,
as was the channel marker, foaming up
to slice our craft in two!

We made that, but
in this bush, who could ever find a child?

"JUDITH!"

A gloomy tunnel in the trees,
a creek mouth, quite invisible unless
you're standing right beside the sandy strip,
thick-patterned by the tracks of hounded bears
who've sought escape here from the hungry flies.
And, here, a smaller print!
A running shoe
has left this faint depression in the sand!

"JUDITH!"

The creekbed wanders 'round a bend,
deep-hidden from the sun; oppressive; still.
I teeter on a rotting log... and then
the rifle's in my hands.
There!
Something moved!

"JUDITH!"

She stands there, frowning in disgust,
armed with a treebranch pole and line of string
and most annoyed to have me interrupt
her concentration.
And I start to shake
and wonder:
Should I beat her half to death
or take her in my arms, sit down and cry?

"JUDITH!"

She glares at me; she's really mad!
"You're going to scare the fish!" my daughter growls.

Little Chicago,
July, 1957.

Trespasser

The one man in a hundred miles
stands on a pressure ridge, and smiles,
surveying his immense domain.
How many miles of icy plain
between him and the Russian coast?
And his! All his!
Now, there's a boast!

The men who gauge the ocean's flow
flew out of here an hour ago,
leaving their visitor behind,
alone in camp.
He doesn't mind.
There wasn't room aboard their flight
for him, but he'll make out all right.
The Otter's coming back at five. . .
and what a day to be alive!

The one man in a hundred miles
studies the pale blue ice, which piles
haphazardly, a crazy quilt
the restless, crunching floes have built
across this frozen Northern rim. . .
just to provide a view for him!

The sky is blue; the stunted peaks

twinkle as April sunlight tweaks
the knife-sharp edges of the ice
now spring has broken winter's vise.
A quarter-mile away, the hut,
a splash of orange - alien, but
the touch of warmth this canvas needs -
sits on one of the smooth new leads
the ocean's motion hasn't branded
with its ridges.
There, he landed.

The one man in a hundred miles
basks as the sun's sweet warmth beguiles
his senses.
Ellef-Ringnes lies
far to the south.
He squints, and tries
to see the shadow of the land
on the horizon...
Lord, it's grand!

No breath of wind.
The ice is still.
The sun beats down...
So, why this chill
which suddenly has gripped his guts?
No danger here.
He must be nuts!
Nanuq prefers the coast, where seal
are plentiful...
why should he feel
so small, so helpless, such a prey
to panic on this lovely day?

The one man in a hundred miles
stumbles across the ice.
The files
of pressure ridges, marching grim
across this desert, sneer at him.
What foolish human thinks that he
can trespass on the polar sea...
a world apart since time began?
This is no place for fragile Man!

The canvas Parcoll hut is hot
this April day.
The man is not.
He huddles by the radio.
The Otter left five hours ago...
two hours or so will see it back
to pluck him from this lonely shack...

His coffee spills.
The pot is dry.
With haunted eyes he scans the sky...

The one man in a hundred miles
stiffens amid the flicking dials
which log the breeze, the rate of drift,
the water temp.
He rises, swift.
There!
To the south!
It sounded like...
With shaking hands he grabs the mike:
"Polar Shelf to L-A-P!
"You coming in to rescue me?"

❖ ❖ ❖

The one man in a hundred miles,
alone no longer, stands and smiles
to watch the Otter clatter in...
and Pappy sees that twitchy grin
and doesn't say a word.
He knows.

We rise above the jagged floes,
the engine pounding out its song,
and head for land...where I belong.

*On the polar ice
off Cape Isachsen,
April, 1961.*

Arctic Justice

This was Aklavik, in the days
before the flying court,
when JPs tried most cases
which were not of great import.
Police Inspector Hugot was
a natural for that,
and frequently was called upon
to wear the JP's hat.

Aklavik's two-sheet curling rink
ran right around the clock
in winter, seven days a week,
and almost ev'ry rock
went wobbling down the pebbly ice
to hoots and yells and cheers
as those not sweeping urged it on
... and swilled illegal beers.

But even in those happy days
there were, alas, a few
who looked askance at sports who curled
and brought along their brew.
And someone blew the whistle on
a chum of the JP,
who found himself before the court,
charged with that infamy.

He didn't try to fight the charge;
the evidence was clear:
a Mountie'd found him in the rink
with half a case of beer.
And so the Justice of the Peace
enquired, as he must do,
"Have you got anything to say
"before I sentence you?"

"Hell, Al!" the miscreant exclaimed,
his outrage showing plain,
"There's lots of times I've seen YOU with
"a case of beer there!"

Strain
was evident upon the face
of he who was The Law
and, glaring up at the accused,
the JP set his jaw.

"The fine is twenty-five and costs
"for beer in your possession...
"and fifty dollars for contempt!"

It's costly, indiscretion!

*Aklavik,
March, 1956.*

Dye Main

Dye Main

At least one Russian missile - maybe two -
was aimed right down our throats, I had been told
two days ago.
I'd duly noted that
among the other facts I had compiled
about this lonely DEW Line site, which clings
to Baffin Island's frost-contorted spine,
two thousand feet above the Davis Strait.

That was before the Cuban crisis broke.
Today, mere fact is cold reality.

And now we sit, the sector chief and I,
and make the kind of small talk which men make
when no one wants to think of life or death.

He's done what must be done; sealed off the site
from all the world outside, except for those
who plot the maps at Colorado Springs.
(The Distant Early Warning Line exists
to feed them data swiftly, so they'll know
that they have seventeen more minutes left.)

For now, we wait.
We do the best we can
to put aside the thoughts of wives and kids
alone, two thousand miles to the south,
and waiting, just like us, to see what comes.
They probably know more than we do here.
What we get comes from Forces Radio
in Greenland and, of course, is censored first.

We'd known about the Cuban missile sites,
but not the Russian freighters, heading west,
their lethal cargo plain in sight on deck.
We know, now, that John Kennedy has warned
he'll seize those ships if they do not turn back,
and that a U.S. fleet is steaming hard
to intercept, if Khrushchev won't back off.
And, more than that, we know this is no drill.
White contrails, high above us, are the proof
that one bad guess could be the Kremlin's last.

"What do we do if the balloon goes up?"
I ask.

Jim smiles a weary watchdog's smile.
"Oh, we have other ways of sending out
"our information."

Pause.

"That wasn't what
"I had in mind.
"Do we have shelters here,
"or plans for getting out?
"Some place to go?"

"No."

Longer pause.

"I guess you can presume
"that we're expendable."

The seconds drag.

Jim smiles again; extends his cigarettes
across his desk.
I light up.
"Well," he says,
"that's probably the reason why we're paid
"these fancy salaries."

❖   ❖   ❖

Much later on,
I wander down the silent halls, and find
the room I've been assigned, and watch the sky
grow bright with morning.
Overhead, the planes
weave endless figure-eights of lacy white
against the cloudless blue.
How beautiful
annihilation can appear at dawn!

And, fate in other hands, I fall asleep.

Cape Dyer,
October, 1962.

The Seasons

Showdown

He was one whopper of a black,
blocking the muddy tundra track
which led to shelter in the trees
and Ray, beside me, whispered "Jeez!
"What should we do?"
(Yes. What, indeed?
Come on now, brain!
Let's have some speed!)
"Let's see what HE does first," I said,
intent upon that lowered head
and bloodshot, angry eyes which glared
across the narrow point we shared.

I'd met the black bear in the past
but when had this brute eaten last?
How succulent we two must seem
if he'd just wakened from his dream,
all winter long, of summer days
and hunting in the willow maze!
His inky bulk sopped up the sun.
If only we had brought a gun!

We stood there, rooted to the spot.
A hundred feet may seem a lot
at times.
It wasn't much today.
One move and there'd be hell to pay!

And that was when we heard the sound
of flying feet on thawing ground
and saw the charging, auburn streak
burst from the willows by the creek;
sweep past us; slither to a stop
half-way between us.
Horse the Cop
was on the job, his fearless stare
fixed hard upon the hulking bear.

I couldn't breathe... and just as well;
one gasp could break the fragile spell
which held us anchored where we were!

Horse braced his legs; his hackles' fur
erect, his curving tail a bow
which nearly touched his nose; leaned low,
taut as a spring... and dared the bear
to try to move him out of there!
He didn't have a chance, of course;
that coal-black monster dwarfed The Horse.
If Rowdy barked, the bear would freak
and we'd be racing for the creek.
All bears hate dogs, as well we knew.
(I prayed that Rowdy knew it, too!)

He must have.
Tense, without a sound,
he bristled... and he held his ground.
So did the bear.
Those red eyes flicked
as agonizing seconds ticked.
It wasn't hard to read his thoughts
although my stomach was in knots:
He'd take us all without much sweat.
One whack apiece would do it... yet
that crazy dog would likely fight
and he could take a nasty bite...

The bear decided.
Nonchalant,
he turned, resumed his ambling jaunt
along the creek.
Horse stood there, tight,
until the bear was out of sight
beyond the spruce, and only then
became the carefree clown again.
Head high, tail waving, chest shoved out,
he trotted to us.
Not a doubt
He'd shown that bear who owned the creek!
And Ray and I, our knees gone weak,
Collapsed, hysteric with relief,
as Horse, in total disbelief,
accepted tribute from a pair
who'd been upset by that dumb bear!

Some people call the Irish setter
stupid.

Some of us know better.

Mosquito Creek,
May 12, 1980.

Lesson

There were two routes to take.

I could go back
a mile or so, to where the public dock
was free of ice, and hope some fisherman
had brought his boat along to try his luck.
There'd been two people there an hour ago.
I'd seen them from the south side as I passed,
but they were merely fishing from the dock;
they had no boat to ferry me across.

The alternate was three more hours of bush
and ninety minutes more along the road,
back to the dock, where I had left my truck.
There was no way around the thawing lake
except the highway bridge across the stream
which drains it.

Three days back I'd hitched a ride
into my cabin on the lake's south shore,
cut off at break-up by the candling ice.
"I'll pick you up on Tuesday," shouted Bob,
above the rotors' racket, as we crossed
the ice-choked upper end.
But it seemed sure
that I could paddle out by then.
I'd seen
the ice was melting fast along the shore,
and all the lower lake was open now.
And so Bob set me down and waved goodbye.

The temperature, of course, began to fall
that evening, and the open leads along
the shoreline had, by Tuesday, frozen hard -

too thick for my canoe to break, and not
quite thick enough to walk on.

Thus, this hike.

I'd walked in twice before at break-up, and
I knew the route to follow all too well:
Eight hours from the south side of the bridge.
The hiking isn't bad if you swing south
and walk the sparse-treed ridges, though ravines
and muskeg give you exercise enough.

Along the shore, it's tougher.
Deadfalls, brush
and tangled spruce, like barbed-wire barricades,
flay flesh and clothes alike, and every bay
can add another hour to the trek.
Yet, surely, with the lower end ice-free
there'd be a boat...

That was five hours ago.

Now, one knee bare, the ruins of my jeans
a flapping fringe about my bog-soaked boots,
shirt torn, hands stinging from a myriad cuts,
face like a road map sketched in clotted blood,
I knew I had to make a choice - and soon -
unless I planned to spend the night out here.

I knew I'd have to strike south, 'round two lakes,
linked by the river, far too deep to ford,
to reach the bridge... and that the bush between
was just as savage as the miles I'd done.
My shoulders ached where packsack straps cut deep;
My .303 weighed more with ev'ry step.
That made the dock a tempting choice... except
suppose it was deserted when I'd fought
my way back to it through this cruel mess?

Well...
What the hell!

I started back, and made
perhaps two hundred feet before I stopped,
remembering I'd spend another hour
of torture to get back HERE, if there was

no boat across the lake.
I couldn't reach
the road before the darkness came, by then,
and in the bush, at two or three above,
without a sleeping bag...?

No way!
Press on!

...Once more into the breach, dear friends...

Oh, sure!
There was no black spruce swamp at Agincourt
and good King Henry wore a coat of mail
these spear-sharp branches couldn't penetrate!

I halted at the forest's edge.
The trees
were not a foot apart here, and the brush
rose waist-high in between, a bristling mess
made worse by fire-killed deadfalls.

Dammit, no!

I started back again... and stopped, and turned
at least four times... and all at once I was
a little boy, alone and terrified!
I plunged into the lacerating spruce
and felt my jacket tear loose from my pack
and floundered on, uncaring, blind with fear,
perhaps a quarter-mile.
Then, out of breath,
I fell into a clearing and collapsed.

My knife was gone, as well, plucked from its sheath.
My shirt clung to my back, and fresh blood oozed
wherever naked flesh had been exposed.
My heart was pounding like a pump gone mad!
I lay there on the rock, too spent to think
of slipping off my pack, and gasped, and then
it struck me.

Here I was.
I KNEW this bush.
I knew exactly where I had to go.
I knew that I could make it before dark

and I was armed, if I should meet a bear,
bad-tempered after his long winter sleep.
Yet I had panicked... totally... because
I wouldn't face the fact that I had goofed
and had to pay the price of my mistake!

❖   ❖   ❖

I reached the road at dusk and crossed the bridge
and dragged my weary butt the last three miles
to where the truck was waiting,
lesson learned.

Reid Lake,
May, 1984.

The Prospector

They found a grizzly prowling in his camp,
some rain-soaked dynamite down on the dock
and, in his cabin, glasses and his gun.
The glasses raised our fears right from the start.

"Blind as a bat without 'em," Shorty said.
Alone out there, he wouldn't have a chance."

The search dragged on, with tracking dogs and planes
and men on foot, but in the Miner's Mess
the coffee crowd stopped asking "Any news?"
But reminiscences kept breaking in
on long discussions on the price of gold,
and politics, and flies... the vital stuff
to people who are unimpressed by death.

"Lord, how that man could talk!"

How guiltily
I thought about the times when I had fled
to miss his oft-told tale about the claims
which, sold and split three ways, had paid the bills,
with something left, perhaps, to buy a drink.
Three years of sweat and pain and cruel cold,
and flies and thirst and grub box nearly bare,
to net starvation wages!

And the grin
which lit his frost-scarred face as he'd recall
his payoff for those years of bitter toil!
And I, so busy with my own affairs,
oblivious to what that find had meant.

On pavement he was lost; he loved the land
though he was ill-equipped to roam the bush.
Poor eyesight and arthritis' crippling grip
had mostly chained him to less heavy work
than packing over rock, or breaking trail
across the snowswept bleakness of the Shield.
He'd been lost once before, but turned up safe,
and he was proud of that, though others thought
he was a fool to push his luck so far.

"They shouldn't let a guy like that go out!"

The hell they shouldn't!
Anger choked me then,
remembering the triumph of that grin
the day they sold their claims; how Alan proved -
if only to himself - that guts and faith
can carry men, where lesser beings find
the going tough, and close their minds to dreams.
Rest well, old friend, I thought, and drained my cup
and left the noisy clatter of the Mess
to think of dreams, and men who find their place.

A tribute to Alan Reid,
lost on the Barrens,
June, 1983.

Antidote

Prospector Hughie Arden shares
a valley full of grizzly bears
on Camsell River, near Great Bear,
but Hughie's had no trouble there.

He spreads no mothballs and disdains
nail-studded bear boards.
Hugh maintains

security a simpler way:
his wolves keep hungry bears at bay.

Hugh catches fish to feed the pack
which stays, of course, around his shack.
Break into Hughie's?
No bear'd try it,
for wolves, too, like
a change of diet!

Camsell River,
July 1, 1987.

Sucker Hole

Three of us knew better.

Bill, alone,
would probably have spurned this tempting break -
the one hole in the fog since Yellowknife -
and Bud and I had flown enough to know
how such inviting traps acquire the name.

Nick, as the greenhorn, didn't.
Nor did he
protest as we three "experts" had a look
and, foolishly, decided on the plunge.

So down we went, and... sure as hell!... the fog
was hanging in the treetops, pea-soup thick,
and we were flying just above a creek
which twisted out of sight between steep hills
that disappeared into the murk above!

"I think this is the Muskeg!" shouted Bill
as, pivoting about its starboard wing,
the Navajo banked sharply 'round a bend,
its wingtip playing footsie with the trees.

"If we're in luck..."

(a sudden lurch to port)

"... it oughta lead us out..."

(Steep turn to miss
a mist-veiled hogsback on the starboard side)

". . . below Liard.
"Then all we have to do
"is. . ."

(Jink to port!)

". . . stay on the southern bank
"a couple miles. . ."

There, conversation ceased.
Bill seemed quite busy with the plane, and we
decided we should let him concentrate.
Our fog-roofed tunnel through the timbered hills
was just about as tight as it could be!

❖   ❖   ❖

A few months later, we were swilling beer
in Edmonton, and Nick brought up that flight.
"I thought that we were goners," he confessed,
"but you and Bud were sitting there, so calm. . ."

And then he had to bang me on the back
because I'd nearly strangled on my drink.

❖   ❖   ❖

That's how these Northern legends grow, I guess,
when idiots who should have died survive,
so terrified they cannot even twitch. . .
and innocent observers think them cool!

Near Fort Liard,
September, 1982.

Freeze-Up

The ragged arrow rose and fell and beat
its raucous way across the wind-streaked lake;
a hundred noisy tourists, heading south,
the dark gray snow clouds hard upon their tails.
I watched them clear the ridge, and for a while
I still could hear their honking, though they'd gone

and I was all alone once more, and filled
with hatred for this land I'd learned to love.
For love is easy when the sun rides high,
but cruel when those summer days have fled
and nothing much remains, except the hope
that, like the geese, the summer will return.

Some say the darkest hour comes near dawn.
They have not lived through freeze-up in the North.

Reid Lake,
October 1, 1981.

Crisis

The kicker spluttered, burped and called it quits
and, chortling in its glee, the trailing wake
caught up and climbed the transom.
Foaming white,
it crashed inboard, to drench my jeans and boots
and slosh, unseen, about the tossing boat.
I cursed the freezing darkness as I groped
to find the catch, and raise the kicker's hood
and free the balky flywheel, which had jammed,
as usual, at the very worst of times.

We had no business out here, Horse and I,
five hundred feet offshore in driving snow,
long after dark, on this deserted lake.

We had no business, but...

Well, we were here,
and it was getting awf'lly bloody cold.
My parka hood was trimmed with frozen spray
and Horse's fur was plastered to his back
like armorplate.

The flywheel seared my hands
through sodden gloves and then...
Dear God!... I thought
about the plug I'd casually drawn
to drain the boat while we were pounding home
through this first blizzard of the months to come!

Two seconds... maybe three... of frantic search
was all I had before the brutal shock
of freezing water hit me; left my hands
two useless lumps of ice; left me transfixed
in agony so fierce my vision swam.
Yet even through the pain my mind was clear:
this time, I knew, my luck had plain run out.
These hands could never row a sinking boat
against the wind and waves to reach the shore,
and soaking clothing wouldn't long conserve
whatever warmth my body still retained.

❖   ❖   ❖

The pain was easing now, although not much.
I wondered, almost idly, just how long
I had to ponder my stupidity.
I'd give it one more try of course, but, hell!
I knew the odds.
I couldn't even feel
the starter cord, much less locate the plug
which rolled about the bottom, had it been
six inches square!
Already, I could sense
the phony warmth which tells you, *Well, that's it.*
Still, there were harder ways a man might go...
And Horse, my buddy, pressed against my side
and wagged his ice-clad tail, to let me know
he understood, and didn't bear a grudge.

Poor Horse!
No seaman he; not in the boat.
He hated kickers.
His place was the bow
of our canoe, where he could watch for loons
and 'rats, and ducks, and beavers, undisturbed
by noisy pistons.
How would he make out?
Would he be smart enough to head for home
once we had washed ashore, or would he stay
to guard me, 'til he, too, had frozen stiff?

I knew the answer long before the thought.

I may have blacked out then; I still don't know
what reservoir of strength I found to get
the kicker going once again, or how
numbed fingers set the throttle in the dark.
I only know one moment we were dead
and, in the next, half-swamped but plowing on,
we'd passed the point and, ghostly gray against
the blackness of the shore, there was the dock.

❖   ❖   ❖

You think about a call as close as that...
and *why* you made it, just as much as *how*.
(Not Horse.
Curled up, content, an ill-made bed
of auburn fur, he slept the long drive home.)
Was it the simple instinct to survive
which pulled us through?
Or was it something more?

Horse shifted on the seat.
One languid paw
reached out, established contact with my knee,
and settled there...

and, suddenly, I knew.

Reid Lake,
Oct. 17, 1981.

The Snowbirds

Blizzards of buntings, swirling, swooping,
burst from the ditches as the truck
slithers along the greasy highway,
windshield plastered with freezing muck.
Naked birches shiver and rattle,
ill-protected by spindly pines;
slate-gray lakes show ravaged faces,
scarred by the north wind's foam-etched lines.
"Winter's coming!" the buntings twitter.
"Winter's coming!"
And off they go,
heading in from the treeless Barrens

just ahead of the first real snow.
"Winter's coming!"
How deadened spirits
lift as the snowbirds whirl from sight,
tiny messengers of good tidings.
Freeze-up's over!
Bring on the white!

*On the Yellowknife Highway,
Oct. 24, 1981.*

Cabin Fever

I tried the bolt the other night
to see if it was working right.
It was.
The solid SNICK!-SNACK!-SNICK!
prepared my exit; painless, quick.
And it was comforting to know
all's ready if I choose to go.

Will I?
It's really hard to say.
I might have done so yesterday
when fragile hopes, rekindled, died
and left this aching void inside.
(I stood there, vapid, cold and weak,
and felt a tear freeze on my cheek.)

Well, that was yesterday.
Today
has come again, depressing, gray.
At least six weeks of winter still;
six weeks to test my guts and will.
And yet... I made it, once again.
Tomorrow?
Guess I'll face that then.

This time of year, the whole North dies.
Each tiny friction magnifies;
each disappointment weighs a ton
and jangling nerves hit everyone.
And winter's fangs slash to the bone
in people who are on their own.

I have no fear of facing Death.
God knows, I've felt her icy breath
often enough to realize
she's in no rush to claim THIS prize.
Now, wakened by dawn's baleful light,
I know she shared my bed last night.

I've memories... a touch, a glance
recalled; some happy circumstance:
two chubby little feet, too long
for baby blankets... raven's song...
the hiss of runners on the ice...
on bitter nights, they can suffice.

But, God! How many nights must pass
before spring's wonder fills my glass?
How many nights of brooding, hating,
the loaded rifle close, and waiting?
How many nights...?

Well, one more's done...

Oh, God!
I need the sun!
The sun!

Yellowknife,
March 16, 1982.

The Joust

Snow, like a blast of buckshot, rakes my face
and instantly my nose and cheeks are stiff
with freezing blood.
I duck and flatten out,
clutching the lurching sled with hands and knees.
We're barely moving now.
The glimpse ahead,
for which I've paid in warmth I couldn't spare,
has shown me nothing but more churning void
and filled my gasping lungs with air that sears.

What folly brings us to this fishbowl world,
an eerie, wind-scourged wilderness of white
where fangs of ice yawn wide for careless men
and careful men, half-blinded by the snow,
can plan no more than thirty feet ahead?

Like knights of old, our armor stroud and fur,
our chargers roaring snowmobiles, we know
that there be tygers here, and dragons, too;
grim shades of yesterday who flourish still
beyond the palisades of Christian faith
built by the missions 'round the settlements.
This is the world primaeval - Nunavut -
"Our Land" to Inuit, yet ours, as well,
and each of us, *qallunaq* or Inuk,
has heard the trumpets on the keening wind.
That call, few men - however meek - can spurn:

To battle in the lists, if only once,
for no foreseen reward, except to prove
that when the challenge comes, we stand prepared.

We'd seen the plumes of snow, like drifting smoke,
two miles ahead, between us and the coast,
its peaks highlighted by the sickly sun
although the crayon-smudge of driving white
already hid the mountains' firm-splayed feet.
Behind us, Bylot Island's soaring crags
rebuffed the blizzard's wrath.
The way was clear
if we should choose to head back for the camp,
an outpost hut at Button Point; a warm
oasis in this desert winter rules.

Pure logic said that was the course to take...
but who hears logic when the trumpets sound?

That was an hour ago.

The first real gusts
slammed into us before we hit the snow,
rocking the snowmobiles like children's toys;
raking the *qamutiks* which bounced behind
with claws of ice that sliced my "windproof" stroud
and chilled the marrow of my aching bones.

Then came the dragon's welcome:
hissing snow
which burns as fiercely as a blast of flame.

The fight is joined in deadly earnest now.
My God, I'm cold!
Our hands and feet long since
have lost all feeling.
Frosted lashes blur
the savage moonscape visible within
the ice-trimmed frame of fur which shields my face.
We headed out at thirty-five below.
Given the windchill factor, it must be
minus one hundred - at the least! - out here.

I have a death grip on a lashing rope
and groping feet find purchase as the sled

rears up, slams down and wildly skids across
a patch of open ice... to smash broadside
into a pale blue slab of floe ice, which
has sprung upon us from the blizzard's depths;
a crouched sea monster, lusting for our blood.

The *qamutik* -long-runnered, crossbars lashed
with rope so they can flex, where bolts would shear
beneath the constant pounding of the ice -
is built to take this battering.
We're not.
Each jarring blow, each carom into space,
snapped short against the towrope or a drift,
forces a grunt of pain between set teeth
and spasmed muscles shriek in agony.
But worst of all's the gale, the whistling snow,
a million stabbing lances, seeking out
the weak points in our armor; spearing deep
through fur and stroud and duffelcloth until
they find our cringing flesh.
Oh, God, I hurt!

❖ ❖ ❖

We're tiring fast; men and machines alike.
The dragon's breath has sapped us of our strength,
although the dragon, too, seems short of wind,.
though far from vanquished.
Stiffly, we dismount,
finding some shelter in an iceberg's lee.
Elijah fires the Coleman up for tea.
Frostbitten Allan - courteous and kind
but, up to now, reserved - walks slowly back
and, smiling, digs into his snow-stiff furs
to offer me a smoke.

No big deal, that...
except he's never offered one before.

Arms flap.
Feet stomp.
The scalding tea burns sweet
and turgid blood begins to flow again,
although the blizzard rages on, unchecked.
The dragon's won; he's held this frozen field

today.
We feel his power flooding back
and we have little left to fight him with.
But as we saddle up and swing around,
retreating, bruised and spent, for Button Point,
The hissing dragon snapping at our heels,
our heads are high.

We've lost one battle, true,
yet in that struggle we've found something more.
We've fought the dragon side-by-side - as men,
not Inuk or *qallunaq* - and the cliffs
of Bylot, coming dimly into view,
seem strangely like the spires of Camelot.

On the sea ice
near Pond Inlet,
March 7, 1982.

The Day We Burned the Iglu Down

We burned our iglu down at dawn.
I was awake, with nothing on,
inside my bag (your body heat
radiates if you strip complete),
vaguely aware that Josephie
was flashing up the stove for tea.
Then, to my vastly pleased surprise,
warm sunlight bathed my sleep-gummed eyes.
Well I'll be damned! I thought.
It's odd...
My frozen hands have barely thawed,
and look at this!
It's springtime here!
I sat up, yawned... and gasped in fear!
That warm glow from no sunshine came;
our iglu was a sea of flame!

That scene from Dante, who'd forget?
The two Inuks, in silhouette,
frozen against a roaring wall

of fire, flames leaping key-block tall!
The leaking campstove, wreathed in flame,
about to blow!

Reaction came.
A blur of motion and a crash
as Guy dove through the wall!
A flash
of singeing hair as Eric bent
to grab the Coleman!
Seared hands sent
it spinning through the gaping hole
hard-headed Guy had made!
(The toll
exploding naptha, close-confined,
could take, much later came to mind.)

In that wild moment, instinct said
we'd beat the fire or we were dead,
for Guy alone was fully-clad.
The other choices which we had
were limited to burn or freeze
... *And make your minds up quickly, please!*

We flailed with parkas, *kamiks*, pants
to halt the leaping flames' advance.
They roared their pleasure as they fed
upon the gas-soaked furs we're spread
to insulate us from the snow,
but, inch by inch and blow by blow,
we beat them back!

Two minutes?
Five?
Who knows?
Exhausted, but alive,
we sagged, half-blinded by the smoke
and steam which made us gag and choke,
and, one by one, grew swift aware
of heat replaced by Arctic air.
The fire was out;
one crisis past.
But *Wow!*
Let's get some clothes on... fast!

The jokes came later, after we
were thawing out with cups of tea,
the blackened campstove now absolved
of blame.
Pure error was involved.
The valve, left open, dripped all night;
the stove itself was working right.
But SOMEONE had to take the rap
and I became the lucky chap.

❖ ❖ ❖

The boy who stood the burning deck
makes better legend stuff, but, heck!
I've learned to cherish my renown:
the guy who burned the iglu down!

On the Barrens
near Eskimo Point (Arviat),
March 8, 1979.

Photo Opportunity

My fingers looked like wieners,
left to boil
five minutes longer than they should have been,
and just about as thick.

My thumb split first,
my index finger next,
and then my middle finger.
All in all,
they really were a rather gruesome sight.

They hardly hurt by then, of course, and I,
assured my useless hand would heal, in time,
grew quite intrigued to watch my flesh turn green
and yellow, where it wasn't bluish-black.
"You know," I said to Rosie, "I don't think
"we have a frostbite photo in our files.
"Let's get some now."

Rosemary got the lights,
set up the tripod; focused on my hand;

got the exposure right and took a shot
(using the macro lens for fine detail)
... and suddenly was taken ill.

That's why
our photo files have just one color slide
of fingers which have frozen to the bone.

Yellowknife,
March, 1979.

Winter Carnival

You see the old church first at Arctic Red.
Perched high atop a hill, it dominates
Point Separation, where The River splits.
Austere and classic in its lines, it stands
deserted now, a victim of the cost
of heating oil.
The new church, more compact,
designed to cherish fuel AND the Lord,
is just behind it.
There, we found the priest,
a cheerful Oblate father, smiling broad.
God's northern vineyard works His servants hard
(and that was in the lines which creased his face)
but every now and then they win one, too,
and Father Max had won a round this time.
"... They've lived in sin for years," he told us,
"but
"the wedding is today, at four o'clock!"

The timing wasn't great.
this weekend was
the last farewell to winter.
On the flats
most everyone, including groom-to-be,
had gathered for the races and the games.
The wind was brisk, but steaming coffee cups -
a lot of them well-laced - held cold at bay
and happy bedlam ruled as whooping kids,
young bucks on their Skidoos and skittish teams
weaved recklessly amid the dodging crowd.

"It's not the best of days," the priest confessed,
"but who knows how the groom will feel tomorrow?
"Today, he's in the mood.
"Today it is!"

❖ ❖ ❖

Down on the river ice below the flats
five teams, at last, had reached the starting line.
This was the ladies' race; a mile downstream,
around an island, then the mile run back
across the pressure ridges and the drifts.

The dogs were going frantic.
Wild to run,
they leaped high in their traces.
Jangling bells
and snarls and yelps and curses filled the air
as handlers fought to keep the teams apart.
They'd be upon each other in a flash
if two teams hit the two-mile course at once.

Bang!
They were off!
The first excited team
exploded from the starting line, flat-out,
the fiercely-yipping huskies digging hard
into the powder snow and hard-packed drifts,
their cariole and driver, half-obscured
by flying snow, careering in their wake.
They hit the winter road.
The sled pitched up
and over as the scrambling dogs resumed
their headlong dash towards the half-way mark.

That was the signal for the second team
and off they tore.
They flew across the snow
their yelping voices frenzied as they raced
to overtake the first team, far ahead.
The others followed quickly in their turns
and Brad and I, well-chilled by now, took off
to thaw out at the coffee shack above.
The ice was rough, and it would take at least
a half-hour for the first team to come in.

❖ ❖ ❖

The leaders reached the island, swung around
and disappeared behind its scrawny spruce.
The second dogteam, driving hard to close,
arrived and vanished too, and then the third.
We waited for the leaders to emerge.
They didn't... and the sounds of merriment
began to fade as people in the crowd
became aware that something had gone wrong.
The tension grew... and then a team appeared,
but not the team which we had watched start off.

This driver was a man.
He headed straight
towards the road which climbed up from the ice,
whip cracking as he drove his huskies on.
A man broke from the crowd and trotted down
the road to meet the driver and his team.
We recognized him; he'd been on the ice
before the start, encouraging his wife,
whose team had been the first to hit the trail.
A boy of six or seven followed him,
but others held him back.

The steaming dogs
came to a halt.
Their driver flipped his sled
onto its side, to anchor them secure,
then walked ahead to meet the husband, who
had slowed his steps.

He'd seen the driver's face.

Two hundred people stood in silent dread
and watched them as they spoke.
The coffee urn
behind us burbled loudly, and the crunch
of shifting feet on snow was sharply clear.
And then we saw the husband's shoulders sag.

The crowd broke up.
They left in twos and threes -
all but the little group around the boy.
Those waited 'til the father, deathly pale,
rejoined them.
Then the man and boy, alone,
walked up the road together, speaking low,
the father's arm about his son, the weight
of anguish dragging at their scuffing feet.

❖   ❖   ❖

What happened?
No one knew.
Perhaps the sled
had tipped and hurled its driver in the snow.
There'd been no one to see.
The second team
had found the huskies on her, and the best
the woman who was driving them could do
was hold her own dogs back.
And then the man,
a trapper coming home, had reached the scene
and driven off the killers... far too late.

They left the woman's body where she lay,
half-buried in the bloodstained, churned-up snow,
to summon the police, while others seized
the wild-eyed, snarling dogs and brought them in,
and staked them out below the flats to wait
the fate which they had written for themselves.
For there is form to follow, even when
a settlement is shattered by the loss
of one well-liked, as this young woman was.
The body must be viewed and justice done
by the police, for huskies which have known
the taste of human flesh will kill again.

❖   ❖   ❖

They stood there, hatred blazing in their eyes,
their bloody snouts, their stained and matted fur
the ghastly proof of what they'd done... and yet
it was their eyes which made my body crawl.
For naked evil burned there; foul, unquenched.
"Come on!" they seemed to taunt.*"Come kill us all!*
"We did it... and so what? What can you do?"
I turned away in horror, almost sick,
and, stumbling up the hill, I still could feel
those yellow eyes, intent upon my back,
defying me to turn around, just once.

Two white men brought her home to Arctic Red,
a Mountie and a teacher.
Brad and I
and two old men were all there were to watch
as, noisily, their Skidoo climbed the hill,
pulling her canvas-sided cariole.
The priest had opened the abandoned church
which, freezing cold, would serve well as a morgue.
Then he, too, like the rest of Arctic Red,
had disappeared.

The sled had reached us now.
Two dainty feet in beaded *mukluks* thrust
out from beneath a blanket which concealed
the woman's corpse.

They seemed so very small.

The old men wept without a sound; their tears
ran down their windburned cheeks and quickly froze
And then they left, as well.
The Mountie turned.
"Will you two help?" he asked, and bent to free
the blanket ends.
He didn't look away,
for Mounties do their duty in the North,
no matter how, at times, they loathe their work.

We carried her as gently as we could
and laid her out upon the frost-warped floor.
She looked so like a child; so slim, so frail,
so lonely as the Mountie wrapped her shroud
about her once again, as if to shield

her body from the keening wind outside.
We stood there one long moment; then we left
and closed the door against the drifting snow.
We didn't speak, as if we feared the sound
would wake her from her dreamless, endless sleep
and, probably, because we couldn't speak.
I felt as if I'd lost a child myself.

❖   ❖   ❖

There was no point in staying on.
We found
a trucker, heading west along the road.
We bumped across the ice below the church
to reach the highway, buried in our thoughts
... and suddenly there was the sound of bells.

Our driver laughed, though he, like us, had felt
no urge to talk.
The girl had been his niece
and his eyes still were red with aching grief.
"That Father Max!" he muttered.
"Hell itself
"would never stop that wedding there today!"

The bells grew faint behind.
The old church merged
into the snowclad hills above the flats
as death made way for life in Arctic Red.

Arctic Red River,
March 25, 1979.

Birds, Beasts and Bugs

Skywatcher

WUP-wup! WUP-wup! WUP-wup!

The slashing arc
of rotor blades attacks the startled sky,
industriously slicing off the miles.

WUP-wup! WUP-wup! WUP-wup!

The steady pulse
of Progress, as the 'copter hammers on,
a thousand feet above the greening hills.

WUP-wup! WUP-wup! WUP-wup!

"Christ! What was THAT?"

"An eagle!"

"Holy smoke! He barely missed
"our rotors!"

"Where the hell did HE come from?"

WUP-wup! WUP-wup! WUP-wup!

The circling bird,
now far astern, wheels, coldly eyes the foe
in shaken flight and, satisfied, resumes
his vigil high above his nesting mate.

Tathlina Lake,
April, 1981.

The Magician

There were some orange trailers
on the riverbank ahead.
"We're coming up on Swimming Point,"
the 'copter pilot said.
"It's nearly noon, and I suspect
"that we could cadge some lunch."
The vote was solid.
All we had
were sandwiches to munch.
Jim neatly set the chopper down
beside the cookhouse door
and out we piled, to see what fare
Gulf's cook might have in store.

Roast beef, three veg'tables and soup,
and ice cream for dessert!
We gorged ourselves with shameless greed
and then sagged back, inert,
to have a smoke and coffee and
to shoot the breeze a bit.

Outside, the camp was coming down.
Before the winter hit
there'd be no trace that on this site
an oil camp had been based.
(The government insists on that.
You leave no stone displaced.)
Trucks roared about, and clanking 'Cats
churned tundra into dust
which permeated everything,
insidious as rust.

And that was when this roughneck
ambled up to where we sat.

"One a you guys the pilot?"

Jim conceded he was that.

"Well," drawled the roughneck, slowly,
"I was comin' in, and seen
"a big, mean grizzly out there,
"an' he's eatin' your machine!"

73

Jim led the stampede out the door...
and halted in dismay.
There was the bear, all right, no more
than thirty feet away,
intent on tearing off the door
to serve himself a treat -
the bag of drying sandwiches
abandoned on the seat.
The bear looked up,
(My! He WAS big!)
annoyed at our intrusion.
He obviously didn't mind
the racket and confusion
the bustling trucks and 'dozers caused;
he paid them scant attention.
But twenty gawking people gave
the scene a new dimension...

He sized us up.
We sized him back,
aware the only rifle
was packed with our survival gear.
(THAT cooled our wrath a trifle!)
For half a minute no one moved,
and then the grizzly grunted
and dropped back down on all four feet.
The odds he had confronted
were clearly more than he would risk
for ham on rye, or cheese
...and dry, to boot.
He pivoted.
One last glare bade us freeze.
And then he... vanished.

Just like that!

One moment, he was there,
a tawny blur across the land,
and - suddenly - no bear!
There was no cover dense enough
to hide a skinny 'rat.
The tundra faded into haze,
monotonously flat.
Yet even when we lifted off

and tracked the grizzly's route
at fifty feet above the deck,
we never saw that brute.

I've gotten pretty careful
on the Barrens since that day.
I scrutinize each willow bush;
mark shadows as they play.
For when you've seen six hundred pounds
of grizzly disappear
into a landscape bare and flat,
you CHECK things, never fear!

Swimming Point,
August, 1980

Melville Island

About a mile from camp, I felt my scalp
start tingling with the thought that I was not
alone out here.
The sparkling sea, the hills
alive with tiny blossoms, held no threat
that I could see.
Nor did the jumbled pans
of ice, a diamond necklace 'round the coast.
But there was SOMETHING here, and I was sure
it was between me and the drilling camp.

A polar bear?
Nanuq, amid the ice
in search of seal, and finding something else?
The August sun no longer shared its warmth.
One thing I knew:
I wasn't going back
the way I'd come!
I'd head on for the camp
at Winter Harbour, four miles farther west,
for which I'd started out. . . and hope for luck.

My tension mounted with each hurried step
across the springy tundra.
Mustn't run,
I told myself,

*he may just be intrigued,
not hungry...*
By this time, I knew for sure
I had a stalker fairly close behind.
I'd halted once and quickly spun around,
to catch a blur of motion; nothing more.
Ahead there was a boulder, large enough
to hide me as I crossed a shallow dip.
I slipped behind it, waited, took a breath
and popped my head out, bracing for the worst.

It was a wolf.
I nearly buckled then
in sheer reaction.
Trembling, breathing hard,
I watched him duck below a mossy crest.
A wolf!
And here I stood, a shaken wretch
who'd thought himself a walking Arctic snack,
when all I had out there was company!

I wandered on across the treeless hills,
light-hearted, parka open to the sun,
and, well behind, my trailmate followed me.
He stayed in sight, too, satisfied, I guess,
that I was harmless, though he never came
much closer than a hundred yards or so.
When I approached the other camp, he stopped
and watched a moment.
Then he padded off.
But later on, when I was heading back,
he reappeared, this time to walk me home.

I made that journey half a dozen times
and every time he'd join me on my trek.
He was a beauty; huge and finely marked
with white around his eyes, his ruff and chest
and big, sure paws on which he seemed to float
whenever he grew bored with pacing me
and drifted off to scout a nearby slope.
He trusted me, I think, but not too much.
I tried to coax him closer with the scraps
the camp cook gave me.
He would eat, all right,
but always stayed that hundred yards away.

The day before I left I took that hike
for one last time, as much to say goodbye
to my companion of the trail as bid
farewell to friends at Winter Harbour camp.
First snow had come that week.
The gentle hills
were endless waves of white, though August still
had two more weeks to run.
The poppies drooped
and fractured at a touch, like brittle glass.

He joined me on the rise above the rig
and off we went across the frozen ground,
as hard as concrete now beneath my feet.
We'd had a roast for lunch, and I had made
two sandwiches.
We stopped half-way to eat,
me on one hilltop, he on his, before,
reluctantly, I moved along again.

I started back quite late... and caught a lift.
Just outside camp, our 'copter pilot swooped
to pick me up.
"Too cold to walk!" he yelled
above the racket of his whirling blades.
"My wolf will wonder where I've gone," I said.
"What wolf?" he asked and, when I told him, laughed.
"You're crazy!"
"Well, I may be," I replied,
"but there he is."
And there, indeed, he was,
watching the chopper climb the evening sky
and waiting on the trail for his dessert.

I've never had
a friend so distant... and I miss him, still.

Winter Harbour,
August, 1961.

The Eagle

The eagle, as surprised as I,
sailed 'cross my clearing, treetop-high,
last summer as the day awoke.
(He must have missed my campfire's smoke.)
I'd heard the beat of nearing wings,
but I was pondering some things
and took him for a raven, 'til
I glanced aloft, and felt the thrill
of seeing, fifty feet away,
the speck I'd watched just yesterday,
wheeling effortlessly 'round
the island near my half-cleared ground.

A glimpse was all I was allowed:
(One man, to eagles, is a crowd)
great wings against a pale blue dawn,
and then my visitor was gone.
But through that summer, now and then
I'd see him circling high again,
aloof, magnificent, alone.
And I, with troubles of my own,
felt for that monarch of the sky,
for eagles mate until they die.

And then, last week, I stopped to talk
with the game warden on the dock.
"The eagle's back," he said.
Said I:
"I'm sorry for that lonely guy."
The warden grinned.
"You needn't be.
"This year he's found some company.
"I could be wrong, but I'd have guessed
"they have some young ones in that nest."

He waved goodbye.
My heart beat quicker
as I bent to start my kicker.

If eagles get another chance,
small wonder human spirits dance!

Reid Lake,
August 1, 1981.

Nanuq

The tracks, close-spaced, marched purposeful and proud
out of the wind-lashed fiord, 'cross the ice
and off into the distance.
They were huge.
It took no expert's eye to recognize
this broad, bold trail from drift to upthrust pan,
and off again to check a mound of snow
which might have been a seal-hole, well-concealed.

The hunters knelt, excited.
Looty's mitts
brushed at the drifted snow, so they could tell
how fresh this trail was... and I held my breath
a long, long moment.
Then, the fur-clad men
rose to their feet again, and Looty shrugged.
The trail was colder than this icy world
and I, the commoner in Nanuq's court
- and sudden traitor to my friends - was glad.

I knew the value of that great, white fur
and how much that could mean where people's lives
are fashioned by how well the hunting goes.
And yet... what price the freedom of a king
whose tracks alone could generate such awe?
For who else but the polar bear, Nanuq,
would, on a freezing day like this, decide
to take a stroll around the neighborhood?

Grise Fiord,
March 9, 1981.

The Battle of Peter Lake

The man was an hydrologist;
the bear, a real psychologist,
and Peter Lake the field on which they met.
Theirs was a struggle to recall,
waged from mid-June to early fall;
an epic delta folk won't soon forget.

There'd been some drilling near the lake,
and so the tech was sent to take
some water samples for the labs to check.
He'd barely had a look around
the nearby streams before he found
he had a grizzly breathing down his neck.
The Barrens grizzly is a sight
you welcome on a boring flight...
but something else when you are all alone,
afoot and in a treeless land,
a metal trailer, near at hand,
the only shelter in your battle zone.

This bear, the startled tech observed,
was rather large.
A bit unnerved,
he beat a swift retreat to get his rifle,
for grizzlies, when the flies are out,
are nasty brutes to have about...
and never types with whom one cares to trifle.
His nearest help, Inuvik, lay
some thirty soggy miles away;
a Cessna'd bring his groc'ries once a week.

Well... maybe he'd been too alarmed.
He had the trailer.
He was armed.
The bear had merely watched him at the creek...

By suppertime his spirits rose.
He did his dishes; washed some clothes
and, gun in hand, stepped out to have a look.
Mosquitos drove him back inside,
but he saw nothing.
Heavy-eyed,
he flopped out on his bunk.

The trailer shook.

The moment he dozed off, the bear
had made his move.
His chinaware
sailed off the shelves and shattered on the floor,
propelled by one tremendous whack
against the metal trailer's back.
The fuddled tech leaped out of bed and swore.
But when he ran outside, there was
no hint of life, except the buzz
of insects waiting for a midnight snack.
He spent the rest of that long night
trying to set the trailer right...
and waiting for the grizzly to come back.

The bear, no dunce, did not.
He slept
and, next day, proved himself adept
at staying near, but keeping well concealed.
His nervous quarry had no doubt
the bear was somewhere close about
and didn't venture very far afield.
He took his readings all that day,
his rifle never far away,
then tottered home, too tired to give a damn.
Exhausted, twitchy, bleary-eyed,
he sank upon his bed, and sighed,
and was asleep within a minute.

WHAM!

Groceries and pots and pans
and silverware and jars and cans
flew 'round the trailer, ricocheted and crashed,
while in his debris-littered bunk,
the cringing tech, in total funk,
crouched, close to tears, his dreams of sleep now dashed.

And so went June, and then July.
And then came August, hot and dry,
when we dropped in to see him with some mail.
"Come in and have a cup of tea,"
he urged.
"I've little company,
"except the bear."

He seemed exceeding pale.
"What's this about a bear?" asked Chris.
(Bear stories, one can never miss
up here, where everyone has one to tell.)
That did it!
"Three MONTHS!" cried the tech.
"That bastard out there, on my neck!
"He's made my summer here a living hell!"

He took a breath.

"I rarely see
"that grizzly, but he watches me
"all day.
"He's with me everywhere I am!
"At night, the moment I'm asleep,
"that rotten S.O.B. will creep
"right up behind the trailer and... KA-BLAM!
"My pans and dishes hit the deck
"and so do I!
"I'm just a wreck!
"He's done that ev'ry night for all these months!
"My gear comes crashing on my head
"the instant that I hit my bed!
"Oh, what I'd give to sleep all night... just once!"

He pleaded, but we couldn't stay
and as our chopper swung away
we watched that lonely figure fade from sight;
one man, one trailer, pocked with dents;
two flyspecks on a land immense...

"Good Lord!" said Chris.
"I hope he'll be all right!"

He was.
They flew him out that fall.
No permanent effects at all,
they told us in Inuvik...
but I'd bet
wherever he may be today,
that man is prematurely gray
and sleeping late each morning, even yet!

Peter Lake,
August, 1979.

Prayer

There was the bitter morning I awoke
in agony, and thought my hands were gone,
and knew what horror was.

And fear, of course:
caught in a canyon downpour, flying blind...
trying that sucker hole near Fort Liard
and finding the fog's grey tendrils in the trees...

Yet those were terrors met where choice was mine,
and losing, just the price a man might pay
for stretching odds too thin.
But this?
Oh, no!
Not with the spring so very near!
Not now!

Give us these few weeks, Lord!
Just one more spring
to climb the snow-wet rocks; to hear the loons;
defend our cabin from the cheeky squirrels
and watch the deep, dark water sliding past.
Give us a few more midnights when the light
still lingers, though the sun itself has dipped
behind the gilded hills across the lake,
so Horse and I - bone-weary, but content -
can sit, remembering all we have shared.

And then, God, you can have him for Your own,
to make Your days as full as he's made mine.

Yellowknife,
March 16, 1984.

(A prayer denied. Rowdy Red put up a brave fight, but cancer claimed him three weeks later. He was 12.)

Mr. Holman

He draped his parka on the stool, sat down
and swiveled to me, thrusting out his hand.
"I'm Charlie Thomson. From Inuvik."
Then,
"I'm one of Mr. Holman's boys," he said.
And instantly I'd sloughed off twenty years.
The Hoist Room bar was gone, and in its place
were tin tubs sloshing and the happy squeals
of naked little boys on Friday night.
Lathered from head to toe, they splashed their suds
from one end to the other of their dorm,
while Leonard Holman, like the Lord he served,
walked on the water without getting wet.

Leonard Holman...

How the mind recalls
that tall young-old man with the solemn face
and RAF-style moustache, and the rambling school
which stood near the Mackenzie's muddy bank.
And Mrs. Holman, brisk as he was calm,
wielding her scrub-brush on those Friday nights
to scour those thrashing, giggling bodies clean;
the kids crammed two or three in every tub,
since coal to heat the water wasn't cheap.

In winter, when their families headed out
to trapping camps along the delta's banks,
most of Aklavik's children lived in school.

Loucheux, Metis, Inuit, they learned,
for those who didn't paid a bitter price:
no weekends on the delta trapline which
the school maintained so they could keep those skills.
Yet no child missed the quarter which appeared
from Leonard Holman's pocket every week,
or solace on a shiny-serge-clad knee
when little boys were lonely or afraid.

The girls, of course, were Mrs. Holman's charge.
They learned to sew, and helped to cook the meals
and - like the boys - grew up to know the love
of teachers who were parents to them all.

I last saw Leonard Holman when the move
which everyone had dreaded was a fact.
Aklavik was to die.
A modern town
would take its place, some thirty air miles east.
And Ottawa, which frowned on church-run schools,
at last had an excuse to build its own.
And so they built Inuvik's hostel school -
a dorm for Anglicans; one for the RCs - which
had non-sectarian teachers they could trust
to teach kids math. . . and leave their souls alone.

I left the North that year, but now and then
I'd hear about the Holmans and "their" kids
(for that was how those students all were known,
not just the seventeen the Holmans raised
when parents died, or couldn't do the job.)
And then, just back a week, a chap I'd met
told me of Leonard Holman's death Outside.
Yet I was sure that Leonard Holman's heart
had never left the delta which he loved. . .
a fact confirmed when Larry told me how
half of those ashes turned to ash had been
flown to Aklavik, to be buried there.

"They came in from all over," Larry said,
"by plane, by boat. . . you should have seen the mob!
"We've never had a bigger funeral."

I found his grave next year, a stone and slab
about ten feet from Albert Johnson's plot,

and thought about the irony which placed
the good and bad so close in hallowed ground.
The town which wouldn't die had raised a sign
to tell the tourists this, indeed, was where
the body of the famed Mad Trapper lay.
There was no sign for Leonard Holman, but
someone had placed fresh flowers on his grave.

❖   ❖   ❖

The spruce amid whose roots the Trapper lies
are rotting slowly, like the sleepy street
which once reverberated to the din
of teams and trappers, roaring into town
at Christmastime and Easter.
Boarded up,
the Mounties' subdivision overlooks
a weedgrown vista of genteel decay.
But there is life in old Aklavik yet,
for life goes on as long as people care.

And, twenty years from now, I have no doubt,
some stranger in a bar will turn and say
"My Dad was one of Mr. Holman's boys,"
and yesterday will be today again.

Yellowknife,
April 2, 1977.